PICTURES FROM A MOVING CAR
By: Jean M. Sullivan

Note from the author

I often wondered what would happen if one was to take pictures from a moving car. As you drive along at fifty-five miles an hour along a highway, there are scenic views that are not only beautiful, but tell a little of the history of the area you are passing through.

I decided to take my camera and try taking pictures from a moving car and here you see the results.

I had the best chauffeur in town, my daughter Patricia and I couldn't have put pictures and words together without the help of my granddaughter Erin, and my daughter Christine who makes sure it is put together and published. My thanks and my love.

Enjoy the ride.

JMS
11/1/2013

Humming "On the Road Again"

"On the Road Again" by Willie Nelson, 1980

Rain on the Windshield

Rain on the windshield making sounds I cannot describe
Patterns on the glass like a covey of birds trying to hide
Tires whine and thump
Lines fade in and out
The storm is here
It is going to last
We will take our time and not go fast

Sunsets

Sunsets are beautiful
no matter what the season
Bright colors glow and fade
Shading day to night

The sea is calm
Waves lap the shore
Sea life sleeps below the waves
Sea birds fly to their nest
A time of day for all to rest

Beach rocks large and small
Driftwood bent and twisted
Firewood for evening picnics
Moonlight walks and kisses

Time

Time is of the essence
a stop will never do,
it is time to snap some pictures
and catch a view or two.

Hold the camera steady
a curve is coming up
Look, look to your right
to see an ocean view
there are rocks as big as castles
all shapes and sizes too

Hold steady,
get ready for a dip
whatever the outcome
know you did not miss

The camera is miraculous
with its telling eye
catching all the scenery
as we go whizzing by.

Brookings

Brookings lies the farthest south,
with fields of lilies white
known as the Banana Belt
the weather usually bright

Fog and rain does prevail
Hiding mountains and trees
Until it lifts and ends the mystery.

The Marina at the Port
Berths many fishing boats
Pelicans and Seagulls
Fly all around
Squealing, squawking, making
Funny sounds

Art walk every other Saturday
Visit a gallery or two
The artists have paintings
And treasures just for you.

Gold Beach

Gold Beach is the next town
The book store is a must
Here you will find a
coffee shop
With sticky buns and
scones
lattes and coffee that is
hot.

Beaches filled with
agates
Shining in the sun
Waiting to be picked up
tumbled and shined
A gift you have in mind

The Jet Boats waiting at
the pier
A transport to river sights
Where eagles soar
White water roar
Even a spin in a quiet little bay
Such fun to enjoy on a summer day

Whaleshead

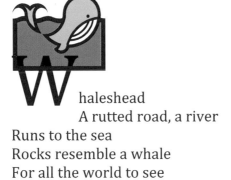

Whaleshead
    A rutted road, a river
Runs to the sea
Rocks resemble a whale
For all the world to see

Stop here for clam chowder
Stag heads and feathered birds
Decorate the walls
A totem pole outside
A viewing porch
To see real whales go by

Port Orford

Port Orford touts a gallery
at a historic 'Rock'
A walking path,
A big wide bay,
Where huge gray whales play.

A cozy new restaurant
Abstract paintings on the wall
A colorful bar with shelves of glasses
hanging by their stems
Bottles filled with liquors, rum, scotch and gin.

A huge cement patio with table
and chairs
For eating out in the sun
Walk out, take your camera
focus and snap
pictures to remind you
to find your way back.

Bandon By The Sea

An artist colony for sure
an "Old Town" that is best
a shop or two to visit,
while you take a rest.

The Art Gallery is filled with trea
made by local artisans
art so unusual framed upon the wall
a fancy tile, pots of clay,
cards to buy and
creative jewelry on display.

The cranberries are local, sold in AThe Factory"
where dishes of sample candies
wait for you and me.
The Kitchen Shop has gadgets which you have never seen
and a display of special coffee beans.

Trees

Oregon is a green State
with trees of every kind
from the tall redwoods
to a variety of pines .
There is ash, oak and maple
chestnut and firs too
everything you need
for a spectacular view
The forest lands
are thick and dense
'til a meadows comes in sight
showing all the rills and hills
where wild animals abound

Gorse

A pretty plant we all agree
It spreads and grows so wild
Invasive is the word that's used
As it takes over all the land
It would not be a big surprise
If it even grew in sand.

The experts are looking for a way
To make it go away
But just like wild pampas grass
We think it is here to stay

Roads

Tarmac with yellow lines
Traffic signs of all kinds
Straight and curving
Smooth and rough
Without them travel would be tough.

Roads that lead both north and south
Shoulder rails to keep you safe
As you drive on from place to place

Coastal Highway 101

Riding along Coastal Highway 101 in Oregon
you find every thirty miles
a town you can stop and visit for awhile

Towns stretch north and south
like all the beach towns do
filled with small boutique shops
touting souvenirs,
fish and chips, grilled or fried
the choice is up to you.

fishing boats, tied up in the marina
waiting for the fishermen
to take them out to sea,
then back to port they sail
with fish for you and me.

Clouds

Clouds are shifting far and wide
Some light peeping through
A promise of a lovely day

The fog will lift
The sun will shine
The skies will all be blue
Time to lift your camera
And snap a view or two

There are rivers and mountains yet to come
Small country hamlets on two lane roads
Lunch stop in new places
A chance to greet new faces

Brambles

Brambles wild and free
Once a pretty plant
But winter came and turned it gray
To sleep away the time

When spring comes
it will awaken
turning green with leaves abound

Side Roads

As we ride along the highway
Signs point to the way
To streets and biways with
Funny or strange names

The roads are not always paved
The ride is bumpy too
For some folks have built their homes
Up in the mountains
So they can have a view

Lonely Road

Driving down the lonely road early in the day
Heading to a brand new town
To find a restaurant
Where we can have a granny special
Biscuits and gravy, a sausage too
Scrambled egg and coffee brewed

More Clouds

The beauty of the clouds
Are such a pretty sight
Whether clear or stormy
Show such insight

Like a painter's canvas
The colors on display
Always something new
As the wind blows them away

Pelicans

Look up into the sky and see the Pelicans flying low
For whatever reason they keep all in a row
They spread their wings and fly so fast
Yet dip and find their favorite catch

They have a river rock they use
A favorite spot that is huge
They land with a belly flop
And then climb onto the rock
They visit and they preen
Then go unseen
And fly away, one by one,
As evening comes.

Coos Bay

Coos Bay, a city of some size
complete with "The Mill"
the Coquille Indian pride
built by the bay leading to the
ocean
and huge ships go floating by

Today we saw two tall ships
sailing down the bay
as the wind caught the sails
and sent them on their way

The Captain wore a red coat
his crew was standing by
entertaining visitors
along for the ride

A cannon was aboard
and soon they showed off
and made the cannon roar

Florence

A scenic highway to Florence
to streets nice and wide
shops and stores
antiques galore
and a new casino
to explore

Old town has a special feel
tiny shops appeal
table and chairs at the bakery door
a chance to sit in the sun
enjoy some coffee and a bun

Seagulls

Brown in color means it is new

This one little seagull is admiring the view

Here is a big white one looking for some food.

Crescent City Harbor

The huge sea lions bask in the sun.
Crescent City, California
Is a favorite town we visit
A lovely ride in the redwood trees
Fish and Chips at the pier
Where these lovely creatures
Bask in the sun
Making barking noises
Greeting everyone.

Slide Area

The earth is always moving
On a mountain side
Leaving baron places
'til a bird comes by

A tiny little seedling
A tiny tree or shrub
Sometimes a wild flower
Or a weed or two
Hope to keep the mountain
In plain view

Bridges

A span
A crossover
Wide
Narrow
High
Low
Steel
Wood
Glass
connectors
To our way of life

Winds Of Oregon

Trees bend from
west to east
along the ocean
shores
as the winds blow
and bend them
even as they grow

The cypress trees
are many
beach grasses are
on hand
as the wind blows
its fury
all across the land

the rains pelt
sideways
in torrents it does
seem
storming, shaking,
bursting in its stride
the car quaking
in a very bumpy
ride

Wildflowers Along The Highway

Yellow grasses tall and wild
Mix with the gorse
A melody comes to mind
with notes high and low
nature bounty dancing
as the wind begins to blow
the grasses are like willows
majestic and tall
swaying, bending, twirling
wild in winds embrace
carrying with it a little Queen Anne's Lace

Before the day is over
seedlings fall to the ground
making sure that next year
Wild flowers will abound.

Still More Clouds

B right blue skies
filled with wispy clouds
gliding, floating, riding high
in winds that abide

slices thin, long and sleek
clouds of roundness
floating free
swirls of color like marbles of old
a little yellow in the center fold

a moving sky as the clouds scud by
changing pictures to our eyes
angels soaring with wings abreast
sunlight catching when they rest
speedometer reads fifty-five
miles gone by
the clouds changed new
the camera caught the special view

Fog Bank

A camera at the ready
looking for a sight
ready to snap but the fog bank is about
It hovers over the horizon
like a shroud of gray cloud
then descends upon the earth
hovering and smothering
where the Easter lilies grow.
the houses look like faded boxes
the trees a silhouette in gray
the needle pines hiding
wafting like a fey
shadows in mystery
no picture do I see
for all my world is
hidden in a colorless world
full of mystery

Meadows

Riding along a ribbon of road
coated with tar
endless miles
a drive so very far

along each side of the highway
weeds grow tall and wild
dropped seedling, blooms are on display
gorse and pampas grass
take over every day

a meadow, stretching far and wide
baby lambs roam and play
within the rills and hills
and open space galore
a break in the monotony
of the long, long drive
a picture for a camera
as you go riding by

About The Author

Jean M. Sullivan is an octogenarian with a flair for writing. She has a unique talent, being able to write on a variety of subjects. She has an uncanny skill at painting word pictures with her poetry and telling a tale with unexpected twists and turns that keeps the reader engrossed.

She lives in a small coastal town in Oregon where she enjoys all the sights and sounds and just can't stop writing.

Made in the USA
Charleston, SC
18 May 2015